Striving and Surviving:

a collection of poetry that I have written that has helped me through some of my lowest points.

I dedicate this book to anyone suffering from mental illness, may you have the strength and courage to continue fighting this never-ending battle.

Hello readers!

I'd like to say thank you for reading my second poetry book and following me on this special journey. This time I have taken my time when writing this book as the first time I published 'Battles with Bipolar' I was experiencing a manic episode which lasted just over two weeks.

For those that are unfamiliar, during a manic episode a person experiences elevated mood, lack of sleep, racing thoughts and speech, increased energy, increased confidence, being easily agitated or experience psychotic symptoms.

I particularly love writing poetry and have tried to include some uplifting poems too as well as poems about nature, love, life and mental illness.

So since my first book I have started on a different medication to help treat my Bipolar. I have started taking Lithium which is a mood stabiliser. Additionally I have started to reduce my anti-depressant Venlafaxine and hope to also withdraw from my anti-psychotic Aripiprazole in the near future as I shouldn't need to take it along side Lithium. This is very much a trial though as the last time I reduced it, I experienced the psychotic symptoms again such as hallucinations, delusions and hearing voices.

Again everything in this book is my own work, I have done all the editing and publishing myself through Amazon KDP. Hope you enjoy. Feel free to follow my Instagram or Facebook page @bipolarpoetry_

Contents

Sam

I went to see a medium and you came through,
animals can talk, wow! I never knew.
You spoke to me and told me you was okay
I wasn't really sure what to say.
I was just tearful but happy you was safe
up in Heaven you have an eternal place,
to live forever, safe and sound with God
I love you so much Sam, my dog.

I never knew pets could communicate in spirit
but you did so there must be no limit,
to Gods such amazing and wonderful powers
on your grave in the garden I laid you flowers.

I also placed a rock shaped like a heart
when you left me my world fell apart.
I've had you ever since you was a puppy,
That day I got you I felt so lucky.
To finally have a Border Collie to call my own
twelve months later and you were fully grown.

In my bedroom I have the photo of Nala and you,
I know you wasn't too keen on her when she was new.
She was a puppy and was always up to no good
trying to bite your ears and chewing wood.

I've got so many happy memories that I will treasure,
they're locked in my heart to cherish forever.
It breaks my heart that you're no longer here
but this was a sign now everything's clear.
In my mind I know there must be life after death,
I cried bucketfuls of tears on the day that you left.

I kept your blanket and toys to share with Nala ,she loves them
her favourite place is under the bed in her den.
The same place you also loved to sleep,
sometimes I think about you and weep.

You lived a long and happy life till almost fourteen,
No love was ever spared in between,
your passing I still love you the same if not more,
your gentle demeanour and your wet nose I'll always adore.

I still hear your footsteps they echo on the floor,
but God called you back and opened the door
to Heaven you went to live again
In Gods everlasting kingdom, Amen.

Nala

A walk out in the fresh air was just what I needed
I took my Border Collie, Nala she leaded,
me along the cricket field as she hunted for sticks,
to play fetch she gets such a kick.
From leaping and jumping into the air to catch,
"shit!" I muttered to myself as I looked at my watch.

"Look at the time, we've been here so long",
I forgot all my worries and what was going wrong.
The grass was hard and covered in snow and ice
it looked like a glacier it was pretty and nice.

I chatted to other dog walkers along the way,
I felt so calm I wanted to stay,
just a little longer so Nala could play
the hills would be perfect to ride a sleigh,

Mud on my boots and Nala had mud on her paws
the light slowly dying as the evening draws
close, as we made our way back to the car
it was so peaceful as we looked back from afar.

My best friend and therapy dog I love her to bits
I would be lost without her she always sits,
next to me and lets me kiss her
when I'm at work I always miss her.

Minced Pies

Baking delicious minced pies takes my mind off my illness,
it's always a good form of mindfulness.
The sweet smell of baked goods in my kitchen
I can't wait till they are cooked, I'm itching
to take a bite of the mouth watering pastry
I need to wait as I'm acting quite hasty.

You will need sugar and eggs to add to the mixture
when they are cooked they'll come out a picture.
I've tried to perfect my recipe, adding just the right amount of fat
then add the right amount of water to the flour and that is that.

Enjoy your christmassy creation
to get it right it takes dedication,
patience is key as you measure out the right ingredients
do this correct and you'll end up with some very satisfied recipients.

Share them with whomever you like
be careful or they'll be gone in just one bite.
Everyone will be saying "save some for me!",
enjoy them with a nice hot cup of tea.

How I Feel

I'm scared of how I feel now
its like how I felt before I slipped into psychosis,
my head feels cloudy and all over the place
I know I said that I wanted a diagnosis,
but this doesn't stop me from feeling this much hate
towards myself, how long before I break?

When people raise their voice it makes me very nervous,
I feel my heartbeat quicken in my chest and I get anxious.
Loud noises from the outside world makes me flinch in fear,
for a while at least, why can't I just disappear?

I've contacted the crisis team and doctor to help me
they have increased my anti psychotic medication,
but its not easing any of this frustration.

Aripiprazole I call it my saviour
it leaves a taste in my mouth, a bitter flavour.
Dry and nasty it feels like I've eaten chalk
maybe I should just go for a walk.

I'm too scared to leave the house
I've lost all my confidence I'm just like a mouse,
that's just dodged a mousetrap that intended to kill it
Am I really here or just here in spirit?

Depersonalisation makes me feel weird
it's scary and I'm almost brought to tears.
The fears are real not just in my imagination
I can't feel anything in this separation,
of my mind and body they feel like two unconnected parts
with disconnected veins that usually run through my heart.

Guardian Angel

I talk to you in my head
I ask for guidance and for you to point me towards the light.
I still miss you even though you aren't here
I notice it more when the days are bright.

I know you loved the sunshine
you was always sat out on your back porch.
I know I need help to light this darkness
will you please lend me a torch?

I've asked the Angels to help me out, you are one of them.
My Guardian Angel, an omniscient being.
You help me to feel positive when `I'm feeling down.
I look up to the clear blue sky and take my eyes off the ground.

Your presence and love is ever so strong,
Even though you're not here in person I feel it in my heart.
You send signs to me through numbers and hidden messages in words
within songs.
I know I'm going in the right direction and need to stop focusing on things
I have done wrong.

I can't erase my mistakes - we are all human.
I can't change the past I have no control over that.
But what I can do is look towards a brighter future.
I can't live a life off others like a moocher.

I need to make my own life and not rely on others too much.
I need to push for what I want and snatch it with both hands.
Thank you for always being there for me everyday.
I can't wait till I will see you again, someday.

<u>I am...</u>

I am...
My own strength and weakness
strong with my uniqueness
weak with my meekness
saddened by my own bleakness.

I am...
Loved for my kind personality
hated for my punctuality
admired for my rationality
questioned for my impartiality.

I am...
Liked for my determination
misunderstood for my exasperation
joyous with salvation
lonely from my isolation.

I'm Just Being Me

Today I was feeling very overwhelmed and irritable,
I kept snapping at people, but I really didn't mean to.
I was swearing like a sailor, but I couldn't stop.
It was pouring out my mouth - word vomit;
effing this, effing that.
I really didn't mean to act like a twat!

Later I went for a drive to calm my mood,
listening to my music soon got me in the groove.
Singing my heart out with the windows rolled down
parked in Tesco car park I must've looked a clown!

I try not to worry too much what other people think about me.
At the end of the day...

I'm just being me.

Rain (Tanka)

The rain dripped outside
on my window ledge it splashed
drip drop... rain damp,
cold and wet like melted ice.
A grey thunder sky I saw.

Wolf (Haiku)

Gold eyes twinkling
Dark fur blacker than coal
"please boy, don't cry wolf".

The Barn Owl

An evening visitor comes swooping past my house
wings spread wide
gliding through the air like a para-glider.
Beautiful creature The Barn Owl
it flies over the fields behind my back garden.
Looking for rodents that hide in the long grass
to catch a meal to eat at last.

Stars Dazzle

In the darkness of the night
stars dazzle and shine so bright.
I wish I could grab them and put them in a jar
Stars twinkle so beautifully from afar.

Feelings (Haiku)

I want to let go
these feelings I can't control
Bipolar kills me

Better Off Dead (Haiku)

Thoughts invade my brain:
"you may as-well just end it...
you're better off dead!".

The Devil (Haiku)

He sees my weakness,
prays on me like a mantis
tries to lure me in.

Hope (Haiku)

Hope is always there
though you can't always see it
it's within your reach.

Happy Place

Run a bath, add some bubbles, take a dip
and a magical trip to that place of calm and tranquillity
where all your troubles disappear and melt away.
It this real or just a figment of my imagination?
That place so perfect and bliss.
Sunset skies, soft sands and silky shores.

For now, I can only wonder and imagine
that peaceful utopia somewhere down yonder.
A place I've dreamt of many times before.

Maybe I'll go there one day...

Maybe we'll go there together...

And live there forever in our happy place...

Let us go for a swim in the turquoise shimmering bay
pick forgotten seashells off of sands, left by the smooth sea
we'll try to spot baby turtles as they make a mad dash to avoid any
predators.
Like the little one I found in Mexico, on Puerto Vallarta beach
where I nicknamed him Franklin and gently carried him into the calm
waves
setting him free to live in the depths.

"Oh I do hope he made it, cute little fellow".
I remember hearing somewhere that the odds are always stacked
against them.

Sweet Little One

Some ask me if I want children of my own one day.
At twenty-seven, I definitely don't want any today!
Maybe in three years time
When my head is more stable, and I am more able
to look after someone as well as myself.

Not enough money in my pocket to look after number one
let alone look after you, sweet little one.
Sometimes I think I'd like to adopt.
Makes no difference to me as you will always be mine,
and together we will have all the time
in the world to get to know one another
I as your Mother, I would be like no other.

To give you what my parents gave me
the ability to be whoever I wanted to be.
I'd bring you up to be polite and honest.
And with that comes the fondness, love and happiness from my family,
that together we could be.

Sweet little one they will love you always and forever
letting you go, oh I would never!

Human

I sit here in my imaginary fairy tale
too scared to leave my tower
like Rapunzel en-caged with her long golden hair.
I've already found my Prince Charming
but it's not just me that needs rescuing.
He needs to save himself first
from his own mind and the darkness that creeps closer.
Stalker, stranger, sabotager the darkness refuses to leave
were both lost in purgatory halfway between Heaven and Hell
were not saints nor intentional sinners.
But we make mistakes, we are Human.

All-Nighter

Tonight I took some Zopiclone to help me sleep
it didn't work I just felt more manic and psychotic
How long does this keep
going on for before I get more neurotic?

Went to bed at twelve o'clock
my anti-psychotic medicine is meant to block
the hypomanic thought's and reduce its strong effect
I know this because I checked.

My Doctor told me my levels were unbalanced
that the chemicals in my brain need to be challenged
by medication to even them out
but now I am starting to doubt,
they're even working correctly.
Who should I turn to, to help me directly?

I've pulled an all-nighter it's now after seven in the morning
I've had no sleep and this is my warning.
That my psychosis could come back
is it sitting dormant waiting to attack?
Like a volcano waiting to erupt.

One: Nil

Even though your body feels weak and sore
you still have the courage to go on and fight.
These feelings are always so raw
it's how you express yourself and that's alright.

You don't always have the energy from day to day
but I believe you can overcome this, eventually.
If you ask God to help you and you pray
that one day you might be better, gradually.

Keep fighting with all the strength you have
you don't want to fall down again, genuinely
try to keep focussed and on the right path
carry on doing things that keep you well mentally.

Like writing poetry as it keeps your mind active
you love the freedom to express what you're feeling.
In your head you are still held captive
slowly but surely your mind is healing.

Chatting to others so you know you aren't alone,
in this battle we all want to come out the winner.
These last few months you have truly grown
God forgives, you aren't an intentional sinner.

We all make mistakes its just part of life
but soon my dear you'll come out the other side
better than before and strong like the knife
you used to cut yourself with and then lied.

Told them you were fine it was just a scratch
nothing bothers you when you feel this lost.
When you feel better you'll be asking what's the catch?
Your hands and feet always as cold as frost.

When you're mentally unwell it's so physically painful,
but you will get better so start believing that you will.
Please stop yourself from feelings so shameful
the score against your psychosis, you're winning One:Nil.

In Denial

It's the time of year to feel joy but all I feel is annoyed
at myself for falling back into depression, my mind toyed
with me I can't help it. I just want to be on the mend.
I'm not ok. As much as I'd like to, I just can't pretend.
These horrible thoughts are really starting to bring me down.
Scary faces I see, why do I see a contorted Clown?

Helpless; these dark thoughts occupy my mind
I can't see the light from that I am blind.
No matter how hard I try
all I want to do is cry.
But no tears fall from my shiny brown eyes
not like when I start to say my goodbyes.

Numb and feeling nothing
I want to feel something.
Anything, be in pain, sadness or terror
this all stemmed from a medication error.
Cutting down on my meds too much too soon
then I am sleeping in till late afternoon.

My hands tremble or they shake.
I am beginning to break.
Not sure how much more I can take
lying in bed, heads wide awake.
With thoughts of a peaceful death
when will I take my last breath?

I don't want to die I just want to rest
is this another one of Gods tough tests?
To see how strong I am and see what I can overcome,
I really don't like the person that I have become.
Fighting every day to be happy, always forcing a smile
I don't want to have this condition - I am in denial.

My Illness

You've robbed from me much of what was mine;
all the things I wanted to do before I was this ill.
You've took all that I had and made me wait in line
to see what the future holds I can't go in and take it for the kill.

You've changed me so much as a person.
I'm not who I used to be before.
I remember what you stole from me, that's for certain.
My brain is weakened to the core.

I have to ask people to repeat certain instructions
I just don't follow them as easily.
This has become a major obstruction
and it really doesn't please me.

I used to be much stronger than this
I could over come any major obstacle.
Now this illness constantly takes the piss
and I need more than just a fucking miracle.

Untitled II

Last night I wanted to wreck this place
throw shit at the wall, I wanted to lose it all.
Who is she? The one with the pale face
will she ever get back up from this devastating fall?

Uncontrolled anger fills my soul,
it's not aimed at anyone except me.
My heart feels blacker than coal,
will these demons just give me a break and leave me be?

The voices have slowly started coming back,
at night as I'm trying to sleep I hear a haunting voice,
just please cut me some slack.
I'm trying my best, this isn't my choice.

Last night I wanted to hurt myself,
to punish myself for falling victim to a scam.
I didn't think of the consequences or my health
I was scared to death like a little lamb,

that's just lost its mother and is being stalked by a fox,
helpless I am to these horrible delusions.
I can't get out of my bedroom box
I succumb to these dark as death allusions.

Dove

Pushed to my limit
can't get out, I'm stuck in it.
I wouldn't speak to you the way I speak to myself,
I'm so nasty to myself I know it's not good for my mental health.
Always saying how worthless I am,
it's like I couldn't give a damn.

Always in self destruct mode,
I can't crack the code,
to healing and achieving,
I want to be better at believing and succeeding.
I need to give myself more praise,
not just sit here in a daytime daze.

I think about my traumatic past,
but it can't be fixed with a cast.
It's not like having a broken leg,
sometimes you can't fix a poorly head.
I went to therapy today to help me heal,
it was hard, talking about what I thought was real.

At the time it seemed so real to me,
I don't think I can ever let go and just be.
I hope my therapist can help set me free,
wave her magic wand and on the count of three,
all my troubles would vanish,
I need to get rid and just banish...

Anything negative that doesn't sit well,
with me, someone drag me out of this hell,
please... I need saving.
Can you see me stood here waving?
I just want you to notice and listen,
see my eyes light up and glisten,

when I open up and talk about things I love,
I set free from the cage, that little white Dove.
She flies off into the clear blue sky,
free at last, she soars in the air up high.
No more tears left to cry,
in that cage she won't die.

18

Fighter At Heart

Stop nagging me to get up and get dressed,
I will in my own time
I know you feel it makes me worse,
to lay around and do nothing and most of the time I agree with you.
But you don't always understand how physically and mentally tired I am.
I'm sick of fighting, not just giving up,
I'm just completely exhausted.
Please give me a break and let me do it in my own time.

If I need a rest day, its for my own good.
I know it hurts you to see me give in.
I don't want to be a burden on you but please give me time to recharge.
The last thing I want is to sink back into a deep depression,
but sometimes I can't help it.
I take my meds and do as I am told
but sometimes these things happen, it just unfolds.
Out of my control, please remember I won't let go...

I'm still a fighter at heart.

The Purge

Alarm siren sparks the start
why do they make us do this, do they not have a heart?
Twelve hours of hell,
Secrets you wouldn't want to tell.
One night once a year
will you overcome the fear?
Go out to purge around,
or stay home, where you think you're safe and sound.

Hiding in your safe room,
enclosed like it's a tomb.
Barricading yourself in, are you keeping them out?
What on earth is this horrendous night all about?

A cull of the people,
a way to rid the city of evil;
the no gooders, thieves, rapists, killers
where does all this terror lead?
The Elite have their purge parties
while you carry out their dirty deeds.

A Father sacrifices himself to put food on the table,
not a rope around his neck but a cable.
he's tethered to the Elite he must do as they say,
be tortured to death while we pray,
for a merciful, quick death.
But it's painful until he takes his last breath.

Can your friends or colleagues be trusted?
Are they going to stab you in your sleep
or purge you while you sit and eat?
Are they enemies that seek to destroy?
To play and use you as their toy.

Screams in the distance, gunshots, explosions
the city is falling with the violent implosion.
Some sit waiting aggressively patient for morning light,
when the siren alarms again to end this terrifying night.

Body count on the rise, main headlines hit the news,
emergency services ready to burst with the queues,
of civilians trying to get help,
while people chit chat and chelp.
Somethings are better left unsaid
you may be alive, but don't speak ill of the dead.

20

April Showers

I seek the days that I'm caught outside when it rains
I want to feel the wet drops fall onto my skin
Next time I'm outside when it rains, I won't run for shelter or cover up
instead I'll stay out a little longer, get drenched and fill my cup.

Till it's full to the brim with rain water,
then I'll carry it
and pour it into some beautiful flowers
I miss the days of April Showers.

The wetness on my skin
the shivers I feel
the cold damp feeling of being free,
being free whilst caught in the rain
this euphoric feeling takes away any pain.

Dissociation

Feeling like its at its worst
Bipolar both a blessing and a curse
I keep staring into space
am I turning into a basket case?

My life around me feels like it's covered in a misty fog or grey haze
it's like I'm observing myself from a distance.
Always stuck in the same old place,
no matter how hard I fight or show resistance.

Dissociation keeps coming back for more
my brain is overloaded and warn out
it's weakened to the core
I will always live in doubt.

Constantly not here and zoning out
I feel like a zombie on the brink of death
I want to scream and shout
but you can't hear me, I have nothing left.

Nothing left to use in my defence
things don't make much sense
to me anymore.

Odd One Out

Searching every moment of my life to seek my kind of people
are there others like me that enjoy writing poetry, listening to music and
nature?
Are they too optimistic about the future?

Hiding in plain sight but never being seen
I've always struggled within friendship groups
feeling like the odd one out, the one that just doesn't fit in.
Feeling like the black sheep or the ugly duckling
a leopard can't change it's spots
so I'll accept who I am.

Does it make me lonely?
That I don't enjoy company.
People drain me sometimes and then I have to take time out to recharge
I spend far too much time alone
closed off from the outside world.

Blue Bucket

Calm tides stroke the peaceful shore
the waves glide smoothly over the sand
leaving behind little bubbles in the water.

Depositing shells along the beach,
conch, cockles, cowries and clams
I'll collect them in my dainty blue bucket.

Kneeling down at the seafront
I'll draw my name into the wet sand with my fingertip
then watch it disappear as the tide washes it away.

Trepidation

Believing I can't write when I'm not hypomanic
words not falling into the page as easy.
Had therapy today and they told me it's me who writes the poetry
- not the Bipolar.
Maybe I'm too harsh on myself always doubting
I need to believe in myself
start looking at the positives,
the little wins and take more chances.
My life is steaming ahead
I'm currently stuck on a train,
travelling in the opposite direction.
I need to jump off quickly at the next station
take a leap of faith and put to bed all of this trepidation.

Jon Snow

Born a bastard, Mother and Father were not wed
raised by his uncle who's name was Ned.
When young, he shot an arrow through Lady Starks chamber
while Brandon Stark was sleeping in his manger.

Had jet black hair this bastard boy Jon Snow
he cannot stay long, for he must go.
To be a man of the Knights watch and guard the wall
protect it from what lies North, and listen for the crows call.

Winter is coming and the night is full of terrors
he wears a black cloak made out of crow feathers.
Learnt how to ride a Dragon through the sky
his parentage thought to be a lie.

A Targaryen, the rightful heir
goes by Aegon, what a burden to bear.
Fell in love with another
who's hair was white as snow; she was the Mother...

of Dragons, she was fierce and strong
not sure where in this kingdom she belonged.
In the end love doesn't conquer all
for Queen Daenerys she were to fall.

Right In Front Of Me

Stuck in the same old cycle of Depression on repeat
when things go well I feel like a cheat,
feel like a fraud, an imposter, a fake
how much longer before I break?
Tears fill up my eyes and I cannot speak
lost for words as tears roll down my cheeks.

Bipolar is my new life now
will I always feel this low?
I miss the highs and the days of being manic
not like now when all I seem to do is panic.
Can't go to the shops alone out of fear
will this madness ever die and disappear?

I hate the lows when I struggle to get out of bed
body aches and pains and voices in my head
they tell me I'm useless that everyone hates me
I believe them when I just cannot see
the person I am...

She's standing right in front of me

Mania II

Mania is inbound I can sense it coming on
before I know it it's come on so strong.
Don't leave me yet, it's not my time to rest
usually you leave me full of creativity and feeling my best
rapid speech and racing thoughts going around in my head
insomnias back and I'm laid wide awake in bed.

My hearts pumping in my chest and my pulse is high
mania don't leave me yet I don't want to say goodbye.
I love being manic it can be so much fun,
leaves me feeling like my life has only just begun.
I feel euphoric, ecstatic and charismatic
much better than feeling worthless or in a panic.

Stay a little while longer please, just don't make me ill
if I tell my doctor will they just give me another pill?
I've tried guided meditation and calming noises
but all I heard instead were the voices
so now I'm laid in bed writing words on my phone
sat up by myself, but I wish I wasn't alone.

Shoes

We are individuals
with our own beliefs and principles.
I am not you
you don't wear my shoes.

Don't compare yourself to me
I am me, and that person is free
free to be what I choose
I know for a fact I won't lose.

I do things in my own time
the little wins I can call mine.
Just cause I'm not where you expect me to be
doesn't make me a failure, I am still me.

We all have goals and dreams
we all still want to succeed.
Until you've walked in my shoes you can't say shit
just cause you've tried them on doesn't mean they'll fit.

Wasting Away

Sleeping too much becomes part of my daily routine
I'm bathing in the sheets, no wonder I don't feel so clean
it's as if I'm glued to the bed
sometimes it's like I'd be better off dead.

Wasting away I just can't escape this pit I'm in now
if I had the answers then I wouldn't ask myself how
how I've let myself get this bad
no wonder people get so mad!

Just look at what you've become
barely feel anything, you're so fucking numb
"do you even listen when we speak?"
"That world of yours must be so damn bleak".

How many chances does one person get
always asking for another one, I bet.
"How are you going to cope in this big bad world alone?"
"What are you going to do when your loved ones are gone?

Lust

Did we get too close?
Have we lost that buzz?
That rush of electric rushing through our veins when we touched
the passion and excitement when we kissed,
your lips on mine.

I miss the taste of you.
I miss the feel of your hands caressing my body.
The look you'd give me, as you'd bite your lip
you'd have me trembling and wanting you
holding my hips, kissing my neck
you'd send me crazy I just couldn't resist .
I still want you, you know I do
I just hope you still want me too?

We both understand things can't be forced
but a love like ours is worth fighting for.
We talked about our future and of things we'd share,
I hope we can go back to how we were.
Reigniting the spark that we felt from the start
just remember darling you still hold the key to my heart.

<u>I Write</u>

I write a lot of words
as it helps me to come to terms
with all the upheaval in my life.
I often sit here in a daytime daze
unaware of what people are saying to me,
it's not that I don't hear them
or that I choose not to listen
I just find it hard to focus.

Oblivious to the time
it often seems I only care about the rhyme.
Sitting in silence
I ponder my existence
wondering where did it all go wrong
where in this world do I even belong?
Not sure where I fit in,
where do I even begin?

I write to escape
and to bring a voice to those that cannot say
how they feel out of fear, resentment or shame.
There is no shame here,
no shame in being open about how you feel.
I don't mind if you aren't happy,
I just mind that you're here.

You'll Never Win

You've knocked me down so many times
almost pushed me to my limit
you always come back when I'm unaware
you catch me off guard,
sneaking up on me like a snake in the grass
waiting to strike as you try to take a bite.

You'll never win - not while there's still light.
The light in me still shines bright
it holds me strong and defies fear
suddenly everything becomes clear.
I can beat this illness each time it returns.
You'll never win - not while the fire in me still burns
it burns hot and fierce, it just fuels me
your little tricks will not fool me.

Scary Stranger

You first saw me as I walked to the bus stop
a simple hello and a smile is where it began
being polite I said hello back and carried on my way.
A few encounters later you made comments about my looks
saying I was pretty and that you liked my hair
if I'm honest I was a bit taken back.
I found it weird since you was a grown man
I was only sixteen you must have been twice my age if not more.
I was anxious to bump into you again,
after you'd asked if you could have my number.
My mum started walking with me to the bus stop
when she was their you'd never say hi
instead you just rode past, appearing oblivious and unaware.
I felt uncomfortable walking on my own as you were much older than me
what does a man like you want with a young girl like me?

Over You

I still sometimes look for your face in a crowded place
I'm over you now, the fun was in the chase
it's clear that you're not coming back
I saw your soul, it was indeed black
there was nothing inside which is kind of bad
you'd think I'd be sad but instead I'm quite glad.

You and Me

I search for you somewhere in the endless abyss
waiting patiently for that special kiss
you're like a rocket that's lost in space
in my mind I still see your face
handsome and perfectly carved like a sculpture
I can't wait to see our future,
together we will be
forever you and me.

Number One

Everything you do
just do it for you.
Stop trying to be perfect
perfect doesn't exist,
it never did.
That idea to please everyone
you've held onto it for so long
what good has it ever done?
Start by pleasing number one.

See What I See

Darling listen to me
don't you see what I see
you're beautiful inside and out.
My dear there is no doubt,
I'll be your root and your cause
I'll accept you and all your flaws.
Every last piece, each fragment I adore
every day I love you more and more.

35

Burden

I know there's some things you cannot control
I worry that you'll let me go
This burden I carry you also share
I can see how much you care
but what happens when it all gets too painful?

My unpredictable moods can make me hard to love
can be laughing with you one minute
then crying my eyes out the next.
I know sometimes I can be distant
but please don't think I'm being resistant.

Our love is special you make me so happy
I don't know where I'd be without you
you are my reason to wake up each day
for that I am grateful and I pray
for a long and happy future.

Just One

Do you ever just sit here wondering about life?
Wondering when it is you're going to die?
A sleep into the abyss
will you leave me with a kiss?

Will you squeeze my hand,
when I no longer can
when I can't hold yours back because I'm too weak
when my bones are brittle and delicate
like a baby bird that's fell out of its nest.

Will you cradle me in your arms?
Telling me everything will be alright,
as I take my last breath
and you leave me to rest
will you shed a tear down your cheek?

Just one.

Do You Ever Wonder?

Where do we go when we die?
Is there a heaven waiting?
Whilst we see our loved ones cry.
Is there soft music playing from above?
Is there sunshine and rainbows in the land of everlasting love?
Will we be reunited with passed family members and pets?
Will we see our Father the almighty God?
I hope he opens his arms to us and welcomes us home.
I hope there's no more pain here in this sacred place.
Will their be choirs of Angels singing?
Will the chimes and bells be ringing?
Or will it be black?
Will there be nothing?
Except silence in the abyss.
Will we ever know if there's life after death?
How will we ever know if there's nothing left?

Invisible

I guess the thing about Bipolar
is that it will always control her
I guess she beats it most of the time
but that small percentage she lets it win
when she's fed up of fighting and wants to give in.

When society doesn't seem to understand
it's accepted but not truly understood how bad it can make someone feel
when her reality doesn't seem real
it's not surprising that society doesn't understand how she feels.

Those days she wants to hide away
it's not that she doesn't fight
some days she's lost in her mind
so please remember to be kind
you never really know what someone else is dealing with
when you force a smile and try to carry on
or don't know how to answer when they ask you what's wrong.

Depressive episodes seem to last longer they are more painful to
overcome
but she enjoys the mania when it has just begun
giving her fresh ideas, racing thoughts feeling invincible
when in reality she feels invisible.

Tired

I'm not a waster
I don't want my life to be like this
I'm not lazy I just feel so tired everyday
my brain is tired, my head feels cloudy
I'm exhausted most of the time.

I have days where I do better
some days I can power through the storm
I tackle the rain with my umbrella.
But today I just need to rest
please understand I haven't given up yet.

Sleep is my sanctuary
I feel safe wrapped in the covers
I can be vulnerable and no one will see
I don't have to face the outside world
on days where I don't feel like myself.

Grieving

Grieving for the past me
grieving for the old me I couldn't set free
lost so much in the process
missed out on so many experiences
friends went missing along the way
never to return no matter what I'd say.
A changed me is the new me
having to adapt and overcome
it feels like I have a new different personality
nothing like my original one.
Medication made me put on weight,
one of the side effects that I hate
fast-forward three years
I haven't really progressed
I've just got better.
At least I've not regressed
I just have some regrets.

This Is Me

My illness is part of me
just like my eyes are hazel
my hair is brown
and my laughter is contagious.

My illness will always be part of me
I'm not going to hide it
I'm not going to shy away from who I am.
I've fought it everyday to not let it take over
instead I just want to live in harmony with it.

Bipolar makes me quite quirky and spontaneous
yet sensitive and naive
but this is who I am
and who I was always meant to be.

Love

Love guides us like shooting stars
flying through the night sky how eagles glide,
although you can't see it you feel it even from afar
it's never a smooth or plain sailing ride.

Passionate and exciting love is enlightening
once you're captured by it, it's hard to be set free
when love catches you off guard it can be frightening
as you say those three little words to your one to be.

"I love you" - longing to hear those words at last
they have such a lasting deep meaning
setting free into the sky, love birds dance
love is such a powerful feeling.

Sometimes I believe that things will happen when they need to happen
at the right time
that the calm will follow the storm
that the flowers will bloom after a wildfire has annihilated them
that it will rain after a devastating drought.

I believe good things will come
but what if I'm sick of waiting?

-impatient dreamer

Someone, Somewhere

Somewhere at the end of the rainbow
is that pot of gold.
Somewhere at the end of these hard times
my life is still waiting to unfold.
Somewhere in this magnificent kingdom
is a person who wants you
they want you and only you.

No time for half hearted commitments
no time for silly little arguments,
I am ready for a steady future
a partner in crime.

Someone who will stand tall with me
and who'll be there when I fall.
Someone who won't run a mile when my cracks start to show.
Someone who will pick me up when I'm feeling low.
Someone who'll love me and never let me go.

Moment

The stars are aligned
and as they shined
you plated a kiss on my delicate lips
soft lips touching me as you held my hips.
This moment I wanted to cherish
but as I opened my eyes this moment perished.
It was all in my head just a figment of my imagination
yet I saw you and you remained my fixation,
I couldn't stand to see you disappear without me
a couple of lovers we were meant to be.
My heart felt heavy at the realisation
and I grew weary with devastation.
It felt so real I thought we was together
now I know you're lost forever.
I'll remember your handsome face
in my heart you'll always have a place.

Lean On Me

It's plain to see that in this world
you aren't meant to cope alone
we as humans seek friendship and companionship
we are beings that need relationships.
We are social creature yet sometimes we seek to be alone
to be withdrawn from all that's going on.
In difficult times we clam up and bottle it all inside
when instead we should just reach out to a friend.
Just remember whenever you need an ear
I will be there to hear
all your problems and concerns
lean on me and I will support
I'll fight your corner and will not abort.

Darkness

Depression just creeps up on you all the time
like one minute you're happy
the next you're falling into this pit
a deep endless pit of darkness.
I try to scream
but my screams are drowned out by this
nothingness that swallows me up.
I'm sleeping more again through the day
when I;m awake I'm trapped in my head,
sleep feels my only escape
but it's only temporary
for the moment it feels good
I just hate not having any motivation
I'm achy and I feel heavy
I avoid all life's tasks
waiting for a new day
waiting for an end
but it's an end that never seems to come
I don't like what I have become.

Life

You only get on life
no one comes out alive
grab each opportunity with both hands
tell your loved ones how much you love them
you never know what's around the corner
don't leave it until the next day to apologise after an argument
smile, smile like it's the last time
dance like no one is watching
sing like no one is listening
make memories that you'll never forget
live life to the full
- it's beautiful.

My Love

I love you so much my heart could burst
it's so full of love for you it hurts
not sure it's possible to love you anymore than I already do
I've never loved anyone as much as you, that much is true.

I smile so much around you my mouth actually aches
I shiver head to toe and my legs start to shake
whenever you kiss me I go weak at the knees
to my heart darling you hold the keys.

Dear Jane

He wanted to write wishful words of wisdom
to inspire others that found themselves lost in this kingdom.
He knew what it was like to feel painfully unhappy at the prospect of
being on his own.
All he longed for was a lover and place to call home.
He'd never written a poem before, he didn't know where to start
but he had this urge and felt a calling from his heart.

Dear Jane

I know you are the one for me
you yourself can set me free,
with all the love I give to thee
then in this life I can truly be.
One day I'll get down on one knee
and to your heart I'll have the key.

Autumn Leaves

It wasn't supposed to be like this
you walked away and left me feeling grey
y tears fell like autumn leaves on a willow tree.
You was supposed to be with me till the end
not ghost me like I was just a friend.
What did I do that made you change your mind?
I thought we could start again, put the past behind.
Maybe I was wrong and I'm the one to blame
for thinking you loved me back, what a shame!
You had me fooled right from the start
I let you in and then you broke my heart.
You tore it apart into tiny little shreds
then tried to sow it back together with little threads.
A heart wasn't made to be broken
instead it was a symbol, a token
to open up to it's lover
a lover that is like no other.

Fly

The higher we fly
the harder we fall
when it all comes crashing down
I want you to know, that I have it my all.

Manic Fire

Mania hits you like fire
scorching hot it takes your breath away
your own actions that you can't control
help to fuel and feed the flames.
Increased energy is like a roaring blaze
you're just waiting for someone to come
and pour water over you to cool you down,
you want someone with a fire blanket to cover you up
to extinguish the fire that burns inside.
You enjoy being manic
but when you play with fire you get burnt.

Sink

Riding the high wave of mania feels good
I'm enjoying the freedom of this up
racing thoughts and feeling creative
writing poetry like it's my native language
feeling social and not afraid,
I've not locked myself away, my usual barricade.
But what usually happens next is I crash and burn
I guess I'll never learn
that staying up till sunlight doesn't help
cause when I fall,
I sink back down a big black hole that swallows me up
that hole is called depression
my enemy and nemesis
it tells me that I shouldn't exist
and leaves me feeling forgotten and lost
it will do this no matter the cost.

Ugly Words

Would you rather see me crumble and fall?
your ignorance says it all.
If you have nothing nice to say
then why say anything at all?
Your silence speaks a thousand words
hiding behind your phone
there's so much I want to say,
I want to argue my defence and throw shade at you
but what good would that do? It would make me like you.
I'm my own person and I'm happy in my own skin
I've been through so much where do I begin.
You aren't setting a good example by being mean
it says more about you than it does me
your hurtful comments and fly jokes are not wanted around here
so, go speak your shit to someone who cares
I don't like your ugly words.

Revolution

We are the revolution
it's time to stand our ground
it's time we stood up proud
we are the future not the past
let's put an end to the old regime
fight till the death
a battle for what is right
we cannot be silenced
we cannot be shushed
we mustn't accept a truce.
I will be the leader
your keeper of secrets
I will carry my sword in my hand
I will wear my shield with pride and valour
I am the justice when you seek your revenge
I am the beginning when you see an end.

Printed in Great Britain
by Amazon

34235157R00036